CONTINUED PRAISE FROM LOREN GOODMAN:

I am struck by the poems of Carson Cistulli.
They strike me repeatedly about the head, face
And heart. Sometimes they beat me with a smile
Sometimes they caress me with their wickedness
I try to get up but they get me again in the gut
As he says, "It hurts at first, but then feels good—
sometimes even better than before."

Carson Cistulli is an actor.
His poems are his films.
I like the popcorn.

Carson Cistulli's book of poems
Is like the rabbit
That pulls the magician
Into his hat
It is like an enormous handkerchief
Spewing out colorful severed hands
It is like the woman
Who uses her naked body
To cut saws in half
It is also like the shy child
Who emerges from the audience
Extending his hand ever so slowly
To feed the rabbit Trix
It is also like the bowl of Trix
That is not for kids

CARSON
CISTULLI

SOME
COMMON
WEAKNESSES
ILLUSTRATED

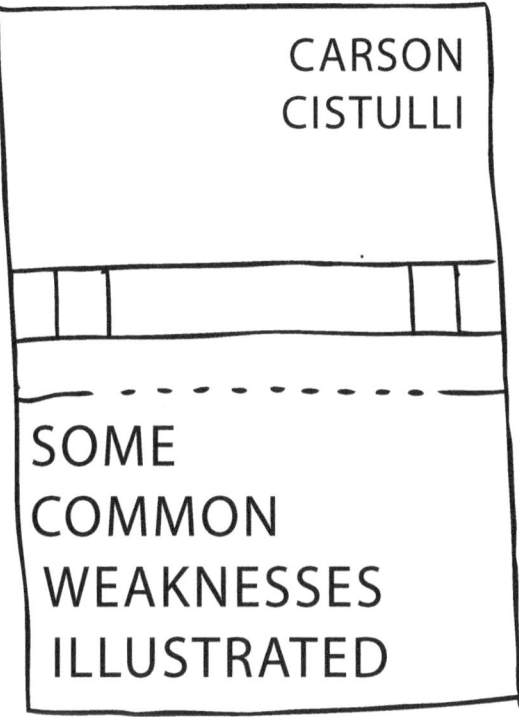

CASAGRANDE PRESS Solana Beach, California

This book was made possible by the Beyonces and Lucy Lius of the Western Canon. And Kali Coles, who refuses to go unnoticed.

These poems have previously appeared—written on the hearts of men!*

*And in the following publications:
canwehaveourballback
Cold Drill Magazine
Free Radicals: American Poets Before Their First Books

Published by Casagrande Press
538 Turfwood Lane
Solana Beach, CA 92075
www.casagrandepress.com
Copyright © 2006 by Carson Cistulli.
All rights reserved.

No part of this publication may be reproduced or transmitted in any form or by any means, electronic or mechanical, including photocopy, recording, or any information storage and retrieval systems, without prior written permission from the publisher, except by reviewers who wish to quote brief passages.

Book/Cover Design: John Berry
www.johngberry.com
Cover Photo: Kali Coles

    Library of Congress Cataloging-in-Publication Data

Cistulli, Carson.
  Some common weaknesses illustrated / by Carson Cistulli.
    p. cm.
  ISBN 0-9769516-1-4 (alk. paper)
  I. Title.

PS3603.I87S66 2006
811'.6--dc22
              2006029768

Printed in the United States.
FIRST EDITION

CONTENTS

PART I

The dandelion was on fire..05
I knew what she knew..06
Juan and you listened to the tapes..07
How are rectangles born?...08
There are colonels getting drunk..09
I was alone but still surrounded..10
The Rue de Bastille..11
Rimbaud and I at a coffee shop..12
Rimbaud and I in a pastoral context...13
That girl's breasts...14
I was trying to buy...15

PART II

COMPOSITE SKETCH OF MY ILLNESS......19
JIRI WELSCH, NBA PLAYER......22
FROM COAST TO COAST WE RUN, ETC......26
from TWENTY-SIX FRIENDS, THAT'S THE SAME AS YOUR AGE......28
ERIK SATIE COMPOSED THE SOUNDTRACK, ETC......31
HE GOT A TATOO OF TODAY'S SHOWTIMES, ETC......33
T'ANG POEM......34
I WAS AN EXPLORER, ETC......36
I WAS WRITING THE ETHNOGRAPHY, ETC......38
I REMEMBER WHEN THEY OPENED, ETC......41
ALONE AFTER SCHOOL IN THOSE DAYS, ETC......43
INVECTIVE......45
THREE UNIQUE CULTURAL ASPECTS......46
FOUR THEMES WITH ANDREW MISTER......47
VISIONARY EXAMINATIONS......49
WE DROVE FOR HOURS, ETC......52
A CASSETTE TAPE OF HALLOWEEN SOUNDS, ETC......54
IT'S 1130A AND ONCE AGAIN, ETC......56

PART III

DIFFERENT POETS' AUDIENCES..61
THE CHEERFUL LANDSLIDE...63
BARELY FROM THE SLOVENIAN..64
POSTGAME COMMENTS BY CELTICS' CAPTAIN PAUL PIERCE
    AS AN APPROACH TO THE CREATIVE PROCESS............................66
MY FUTURE IN BUSINESS...67
A LOREN GOODMAN POEM I WROTE TO AIMEE LEDUC
FROM FOURTH GRADE YESTERDAY...68
AMBASSADOR TO A LAVA LAMP, ETC...69
TWO SONNETS...70
from THE CONTEMPLATIVE'S JOKE BOOK..72
POPULAR SUPERSTITIONS...73
EXCUSE MY PURE PRAYER...74

This is just like television, only you can see much further.
—Chance the Gardener, *Being There*

PART ONE

The dandelion was on fire right in my face. I came this close to saving the world, but now I'm the last one left. Don't all Slovenes have this dream? Anyway, I spend all morning teaching English to a diamond. At noon I roam around in the liquor stores or rummage through girls' top drawers. By evening I feel elderly and write songs to be played at my funeral. Obviously, there's no one to play them. But this is the dream, and this is the way it happens.

I knew what she knew, that beards can grow on furniture if you aren't careful. That living wills have legs and hate audibles. Anyone who disagrees hasn't heard this poem is highly symbolic. Here's some more. That leaves burn at the slightest nuzzle of a carport. That fire itself is mustard inseparable from its mother. In the Americas you can make it if you're a prostitute. In fact, this poem deals with that very issue.

Juan and you listened to the tapes of Buddy Holly executing French monarchists. The muffled voices seemed to be reading this afternoon's sports scores. In the driveway a van was pulling up to return missing luggage. But they'd made a mistake: these bags contain the leftovers of Shaker culture, yours are in Duluth getting frenched. "More wine please," you say to the neighbor children who play kickball on the mountain. Juan is close to discovering the sun's mouth. And in your pocket you find the tattered letter of a Union soldier. "Dear My Sweet Hibiscus Flower," it begins. "I saw you in the supermarket, by the bathroom cleansers. In my line of work that's as much as one can ask for." And it's written in your own winding script, and it's dated only forty seconds ago.

How are rectangles born? And also, how are eaglets made? Do you predict what I'm about to say in these poems, or do you just not care? Did I tell you the size of my wound? At its widest point, it's the size of the wilderness. Someone was dicking around in there. They left pieces of their lunch in my wound. Just know that when I say "now" I mean your "now" and not mine. I live in a poem while you live in a neighborhood or portico or in underwear from the drugstore. There's no telling how great you are or will become. Of course, that's me being optimistic.

There are colonels getting drunk at high school dances all over the county. And there are microorganisms fighting over toys. When I'm finally happy I'll write you letters that say: "Dear [your name here], Hammurabi's Code isn't half bad in my eyes, how is it in yours?" To which you'll reply: "Dear [my name here], Your car is blocking mine in the driveway." And after all that is settled I will pet Pavlov's dog. I will circumspect a girl in a tight shirt. I will join the army for a few laughs. As you can see by this essay, my options are basically limitless and I am smiling in the photographs published here. If there is one requirement it is to be alive, and I mean that in as many ways as possible.

I was alone but still surrounded by close friends. "Is this some sort of logic problem?" asked one of my students as he drank himself to the point of needing another drink. "No," I replied, but of course I was lying. My wife was beside me. She looked like a sad female magician whose tricks aren't all that impressive. "Why a 'female' magician?" she asked. "Why not just 'a magician'?" The answer would take days to explain and then even more to interpret. I didn't have that kind of time: this was the future and on Venus, where the day is over 5000 hours. The sun setting is like a major tragedy, you're enveloped in so much dark and cold. "Which reminds us constantly of our weak mortal condition," wrote one of the masters years before any of this happened. And for him, traveling was probably just a foot this way, a foot that.

The Rue de Bastille ran right up to the orphanage where I lived as a small child. I could be found half the time shaking my fists at God, and the other half lifting the skirts of some whore or another. O tempests in my mind! O spiders that called my armpits home! My caretakers beat me with their King Jameses. "Take that for writing poems!" they'd say. "Take that for cursing His name!" Somewhere abroad and a hundred years later, you're crying for me in a nice liberal cafe where they wash your dishes. Lot of good that does me!, who must lick the soles of a bully's shoes, who must run the streets all night, trying to escape the perimeter of my own disfiguring shadow.

Rimbaud and I at a coffee shop, writing poems. "There are taxes to do," he says, and I agree. March 9th, March 10th: where do the days go?

Rimbaud and I railing against Beauty at a little-known brasserie. He's dressed up in the blood of his enemies. I'm scratching at the sores in my crotch. As the women walk by they try to french us, but we don't permit them access to our mouths-of-rank-deed.

Rimbaud and I at the symphony orchestra. He smashes the head of a violinist. I place the conductor's baton in my pants. Is this Mahler they're playing, or a work of the avant-garde? "We are visionaries, not simply rebels," I explain, but they possibly did not see me.

Once more, Rimbaud and I at a coffee shop. I rape the barista, much to her enjoyment. Rimbaud writes a poem that is pensive in tone. "There are the taxes to do," he reminds me. Ah yes! 1872, 2002, every other year: poets of mild manners are not real poets—do not forget to have a savior!

Rimbuad and I in a pastoral context, comparing and contrasting scarlet and black wounds. "I was created to destroy, if you know what I mean," he says. To which I reply: "I was just about to say the same thing." The only thing more beautiful than a beautiful thing is a beautiful thing's ruin: that's the basic message of all I say. As for Rimbaud, he's off to dig through compost with bare hands, to piss in the cups of the middle class. Metaphysical pirouettes? What's that? I'm just whispering these words to my cupped hands. And the cancer that'll kill me is from this hot sun right now.

Once again, Rimbaud and I in a pastoral context. The flowers bellowing our names. The insects annoying us like women. What region of the mind makes me do this? What is the constant landscape I paint with eyes closed? I don't know. Hey, darkling bird, I hope you die. I'll be happy to outlive you, outlive everything. Let children lie in my path so I can kick them. My trail is full of vanquished limbs and the twice-broken necks of saviors.

That girl's breasts distracted everyone at the baseball game. The umpire frequently mistook the count. The pitcher had no cares as to the location or delivery of his pitches. Nor did the batters appear to mind striking out at all. As a sidenote, a TV colorman did make one insightful commentary, as follows: "Though I owe much of my life's happiness to the splendor of this beautiful and honored game, there are times when we submit to a force beyond our control, no matter how it might compromise our relationship to those things we hold dear. I confess that, at this point, I am entirely invested in the magnanimity of this woman's bosom and have no further concerns other than just to stare at her chest for as long as I live. And, if 'as long as I live' is only for the next minute, it'll have been worth it, for this moment could span ages if it were judged in terms of truth and beauty, the meanings of which I have just now understood."

I was trying to buy a train ticket, but the ATM wouldn't work. Or perhaps I wasn't working it correctly. Regardless, everyone's eyes were on me in that funny-looking rail station. Really, it looked more like a bedroom—indeed, I think it was one. Not mine, of course. Mine has more paintings and fewer trains. Ha! How about that: "fewer trains," I said. I must have quite a sense of humor to make such outrageous propositions.

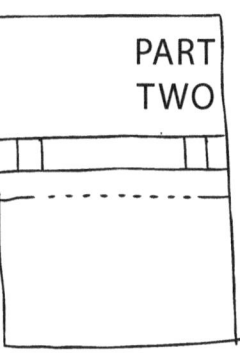

COMPOSITE SKETCH OF MY ILLNESS

1

I'm separate from the author. Like a moth, I have fur on my back. Like a lawyer, I'm the product of two quick scams. I can't see beyond the poem in which I'm trapped. Like the dead, I have no heart. Like an athlete, I'm optimistic. Although this paragraph is ending, something doesn't end. I'll give you one guess.

2

The parable started with a Spanish inventor stapled to an ad for make-up. It ended with the discovery of magnetite in the ear of a philosopher. The decades in between feature a legless chair, a thoughtless son, and only one Super Bowl champion: your New England Patriots.

3

He was made handsome by the light of the toll plaza. Passing through the night beside Iowa's premier designer, his beard grew an inch every minute, and the place he'd come from seemed to call his name: Richard Brinsley…

4

He spent his entire adult life searching for what rhymes with "decaf." The answer could only be found by asking an arrhythmic child. At some point the eye becomes a mirror and not an eye. Its possessor sweats profusely and cites his own work when answering questions about the existential dilemma.

5

The plot took place. A man in a suit washed his car from fifty feet away. A bluebird landed on a Caesar salad without public recourse. From our knees we saw Boston, but from our backs we saw her breasts cascading down. By "we" I mean myself plus everyone in Tokyo. That's the thing about Tokyo: I love them, but I'm not in love with them.

6

Silence is a business, you better believe it. There's a sale on cerebral cortexes. You never thought you'd see that word pluralized, but it happens—to Ramirez, and to Jesus—and that's all I can say on the topic of "What are you thinking right now, Carson?"

7

I took Latin in a small room. The parachute opened before the instructions said. When you can taste your own lungs, what does that mean?

8

I epoxied myself to a ruins. The mystics came to browse my pockets. Heaven lurked more closely than usual. My bones were crumbling one by one. Read on if you want, but it only gets worse.

9

My nephew was the lawyer who represented Death. Man, people are really trying to sue these days. Take this bus driver, for example. He accidentally sat in the ejector seat. Now he parts his hair on all different sides. This is happening all the time, and we don't even know. And Christ won't even stop by for a little savioring.

10

I was in preparation for an air conditioner contest. You sit in a cold room and give a lecture on the human heart. My secret is to slip drugs into my socks. I radiate the principles on which the universe was founded: if it's close, embrace it; if it's far, blow it up. Of course, the opposite is true and also will suffice.

11

Don't let me see you in your miniskirt of emeralds. I'll tell you the equation. Emeralds equal my eyes and your skirt equals the entire world to me. The entire world to me equals your pubis. It's convoluted, hard to prove, and signifies nothing: just like a man who rushes after little girls in the amber light. I might've said this before. And also, I might've said this again.

JIRI WELSCH, NBA PLAYER

1

I'd just finished my poem for Jiri, the room filling with the light off a newspaper. The TV was turned to a commercial for medication that helps you throw a tighter spiral. Then it was turned to a cable channel wholly dedicated to naming your children. My room was festooned with the entrails of other failed poems: this one about the patron saint of internet browsing, another one to the government official in charge of two thumbs up.

2

When I finished my poem for Jiri, I realized I'd completely forgotten the videos. One was an instructional tape on how to hit the cold-blooded shot. The other was a comedy about a guy who dances with the whole school as back-up. Then the place was closed when I got there. "I needed that like a hole in the head," I told my girlfriend when I came home. To which she replied: "My name is Kali, so put that in your poem, for chrissakes."

3

When I finished my poem for Jiri, I had bogeys at six o'clock. Then, after some clever maneuvering, they were back at one. "Man that was a fast seven hours," I told my wingman back at the base. To which he replied: "You're a regular time-traveler!" From then on, that was always a big joke between us. Later, he even read my poem for Jiri and gave some clever suggestions. Interestingly, he was writing his own poem—for Cavs big man Carlos Boozer, whose aura or something had always really impressed me.

4

I finished my poem for Jiri at noon and by 3PM was already back on the coast. The waves rolled in like answers to the SAT. The sky was overcast as Emily Dickinson's wardrobe. In one poem, she uses the phrase "body of work" in a suggestive manner. In another, she uses her own hair as an escape mechanism. "That would take years to learn," I said after I read it the first time. Then I went and taught my beard to speak French. Even as I shaved it later on, you could hear the diminutive "mon dieu"s ringing and ringing out from the vicinity of my newly-shorn chin.

5

When I finished my poem for Jiri, I read that Tomaz Salamun one about the Rhode Island-Connecticut basketball game. He goes on to describe the three-point shot as "the period to end all sentences." After that, I read an account of someone's normal day, except it's written in Middle English. In it, some rather intelligent armies clash by night: no you are, Matthew Arnold! The waves outside were like tasteless suppers. The sky was overcast as hotel/motel management. The painter in the story was just beginning a new series—it's of women and men stricken with heartburn, searching over these high plains for effective relief, stat.

6

When I finished my poem for Jiri, I was to going to leave the café and play video games. Instead, I stayed there and thought about Vancouver while some girls in back celebrated. Later, I was supposed to attend a party, but instead fixed a tire that I myself had flattened. When would my fave pen run out?, I wondered. When would the winning streaks end? Outside, the waves rolled in like introductory offers. The sky was overcast as tiresome metaphors. An actor played all the parts himself to a theater of empty seats. Rapturous applause. Unanimous victory. Anyone could be this country's next great general.

7
When I finished my poem for Jiri, I found myself in someone else's poem entirely. First, I was at a World Series that never happened, deliberately spilling beer on my own self. Next, I was at the abandoned air strip of an Arctic village. "Hello," I said to the natives, but they only greeted me with looks of woe and sorrow. Then it changed the subject abruptly to where I was an academic fluent in German. "Gutentach, Lebensweisheitspielerei": what was I saying? I don't know about that, but the assembly I was addressing loved it. Vigorously they applauded as I went backstage, where I noticed the part in my hair had changed and was mortified.

8
When I finished my poem for Jiri, I found the part in my hair had changed from left to right. Strangely, it was not a symbol at all— but only an everyday occurrence. Under it, my face looked panic-stricken and screwed-up, war-torn and history-laden. Turning to my poems, I saw they were all signed "Anon," "Anon," "Anon." My phone number slowly disappeared from the book. And even now I saw I had a cleft chin, a cleft lip, even a cleft note. Grasping the conductor's baton, I turned to the orchestra, which waited with holy optimism. They needn't have even known their instruments that day, they were so rife with inspiration—or, literally, a "breathing into."

9
When I finished my poem for Jiri, I also wrote one like Hesiod, Theogony. In it, "The God of Breakfast Cereals wedded the Goddess of Commuter Radio, who then bore the Gods of Electric Razor Technology and Business Casual along with the Goddesses of That Not-So-Fresh Feeling and also Fast-Acting Relief." Later on, "The God of Post-Game Analysis, along with his cronies Empty Rhetoric and Retarded Catch-Phrase, raped the Goddess of Acute Observation, who then bore The God of My Creative Powers, a sickly waif tormented constantly by Nervous Temperament and Boston's Offensive Woes." Outside, the waves rolled in like scenic end table. The sky was overcast as women, conspirators in causing difficulty.

FROM COAST TO COAST WE RUN, ETC

From coast to coast we run,
excited by the potential of certain medications—
one that helps you read Ulysses without wanting to die,
one that gives you the strength
to say "Smash Hit" fives times fast.

A sitcom's debuting tonight—
about an explorer lost in a supermarket,
looking for the aisle marked New Worlds.

Dave Berman, they're canonizing your On the Nature of Tennis,
but not you're The Art of Poetry,
because it's written on the back of a cocktail napkin
now buried at the town dump.

"I think I'll be remembered as a Renaissance poet," you write in it,

"but only by my mother,

and her mother before her."

And then there's the story of the foreign poet,
forgotten in his own time
and all the times after that.

About to die, he withdrew all his money
and bought what he could of an artificial heart.

Turning to his wife, he said, "Put this in me," and fell asleep.

Twenty years later,
the half of heart lay on the mantle
as she listened to a Teach-Yourself-English record
dug up from the attic.

"I run, you run, she runs," said the voice on the record.
"I run, you run, she runs," she repeated,
on one of those cloudless days
when you can see that far.

from TWENTY-SIX FRIENDS, THAT'S THE SAME AS YOUR AGE

*   14   *

Am I a French poet who writes poems twenty years too early?

Am I a Chilean who instructs rocks and has only praise for bee stings?

Or am I an American who makes himself in delusions?

Who patents insults of the perfect technique?

*   18   *

Does he call one dog Rimbaud and the other Holderlin?

Does his beard-on-fire escape the perimeter of our foresight?

And does he read the jogger's manual as he converts from religion to religion?

*   19   *

How far does Death see?

To the city from the country?

To Paris from Baltimore?

And does it alter his voice's fatefulness?

And does it make my dreams deshroud themselves?

*   20   *

Where there's beer is there also the alarum within of my personality?

Do you say, "Where's that shite-ing poet?" as I walk my internal concourses?

Or do you write my epithet on all the walls to embarrass me out of existence?

*   21   *

Am I a linguist of self-translation?

Do I placate my inner selves just to find meaning?

Does an orange eat you, or you it?

And how would you know unless a child tugged your sleeve?

*   22   *

Every poem is lonely and en route, you say?

Did you say that, poet Paul Celan?

Or was it the hush in my heart finally standing up for itself?

*   25   *

Is this the story of the left and right hands?

In love, but always in opposing quadrants?

And hiding their secret desires while we sleep in wandering beds?

*   26   *

When you turned 26, did it feel like anything?

Or did the day pass quietly?

Like a fly in the other room you'll never even see?

Like those who walk with you, but always one street down and one street over?

ERIK SATIE COMPOSED THE SOUNDTRACK, ETC

Erik Satie composed the soundtrack to this moment:

a housefly circling the room
waiting for clearance to land,

the clouds coming inside uninvited,

the books all reading themselves aloud
but never stopping to listen.

On a couch in the corner
one stripper explains to another
her definition of the word "relationship"

before the second responds with a stirring account
of the first westward expeditions
during which men would often consume
"up to ten pounds of meat a day."

In the cupboard, the pot calls the kettle "black"
but only with the understanding of what this signifies
from a postcolonial perspective.

In the portrait on the wall
I'm seated in a wicker chair bought at a store
whose radio ads urged one to
"go wild at Wicker Warehouse."

The VCR in my right hand
signifies my attempt to record everything

while the mitt on my left represents nothing,
other than this was painted between innings
of a heated company softball game.

And that look on my face is the one you get
after you bang your elbow on something hard,
and it hurts at first, but then feels good—
sometimes even better than before.

That's the face I made most of the time
during my multiple stints on the DL
from the myriad heartbreaks I suffered
at the hands of ambassadors' daughters
and a world only understood
by equations-to-be-named-later.

I spent the majority of my life
in the room where this portrait hangs,
watching newsflashes via satellite
and playing board games that just hinted
at a reality that lie beyond.

It was a way to get from morning to night
without the nagging pain or messy spills
that sometimes plague our daily life

and remains the cheapest, easiest form of a time travel
never addressed in science fiction—

the one where you wait for time
like a sharply hit groundball,
as opposed to rushing the play
and risking an error
in a game that's tight from start to finish
and decides the fate of a long, long season.

HE GOT A TATOO OF TODAY'S SHOWTIMES, ETC

He got a tattoo of today's showtimes.
The eagle has a modus operandi.
Believe it or not, he said.
He could go either way on that magazine issue.
An ant like him start a revolution?
Now even alligators demand big contracts.

T'ANG POEM

A flock of martinis
flies across the horizon

the dinner bells
whisper today's exploits:

"the revolution is contagious
someone set the library on fire

Bonnie and Clyde are
boyfriend-girlfriend in hell"

in the Great Hall of Stereo Parts
the alarm clock digits
alight the whole scene:

a mouse
composing social tracts

a fly
beheading its contemporaries

and a businessman
espousing an absolute faith
in the power and glory
of highway gas mileage

in the corner of the picture
I wait beside the guillotine

the sun in my back pocket

and a threat of pending snowblindness
not in tomorrow's forecast
but at some point in all of our futures
like a rough draft opus posthumous

I WAS AN EXPLORER, ETC

I was an explorer in an imagined territory,
traversing deserts of unparalleled size,
alternately making peace and then warring with the natives
who appeared suddenly from behind rocks or small shrubs.

Always, I kept a journal with me
to record events of some significance,
or of none whatsoever.

"Day 112—," I wrote, "detected a second moon
exactly like the first,
except for a large tear it seems to shed perpetually,
from so much neglect, I'd assume."

Or: "Day 468—said the word 'finger' until it no longer made sense.
Now, looking at my fingers, I have no idea what they are,
except they're wildly useful
for writing letters to my earliest ancestors."

When asked how I found my way to this place,
I had no answer other than to fall asleep at once.
And with regard to my escape,
it was all a bit hazy,
although I distinctly remembered a certain someone in dark glasses
holding a wanted poster with my face on it.

"Have you seen this man?" he asked,
laughing like a live studio audience.

But when I opened my mouth,
I didn't know which answer to give,
because either "yes" or "no"
would tell only half the truth.

Until, next thing I knew,
I was waking up in the proximity of a hangover,
the trees outside undressing themselves,
and a mirror in the corner of the room,
which, in the midst of a deep religious anxiety,
was capable only of self-reflection.

I WAS WRITING THE ETHNOGRAPHY, ETC

I was writing the ethnography of an obscure Midwestern people
whose language was composed entirely
of the sound effects and background music
from late twentieth century video games.

"When they make the sound of an RPG,
it signifies a desire for solitude and diet cola," I wrote.
"Whereas, if they hum the theme song
from any of the Madden games,
it means they'd like to share a beer with you
and reminisce about good, old days.

"Of course, it goes without saying,
their language is inseparable from their religion,
and their religion from their system of government."

As I finished Chapter 8: War as an Alternative to Sport,
a newsflash interrupted me
concerning the discovery of a new social disease
transmitted only at the instance of a firm handshake
coupled with the phrase,
"It's been a pleasure doing business with you."

The effects of the condition
were apparently detected only much later in life,
at the moment when one looked back on things
and concluded it was all for naught,
except for a walk-off homer here and there
on the otherwise bleak landscape of existence.

At that point, it was so quiet you could hear a pin drop.
Going downstairs, I found my mother at the kitchen table
surrounded by a floor covered only in pins.

"These help you test volume," she said,
bending over to pick them up again.

The twins were by the stove,
conducting an experiment to see what'd happen
if you cooked pasta for one second longer
than the directions on the box suggested.

"They appear to grow sad,
as reflected by their whispers,
which only I can hear," said one.

To which the other added:
"Yes, it's true, I can't hear the whispers.
I'm the dumber twin."

We were expecting our neighbor, the oversensitive rape victim,
but she was late as usual,
undoubtedly lecturing small groups of college girls
on the perils of sex and dating.

"Now I know how those Sabine women felt,"
she'd said on one occasion.
"Or even Leda, although I'm not sure if swans count."

It was getting late,
the neighborhood filling with the blue glow of televisions
tuned to sitcoms and reality shows.

We talked about the phrase "between the wars."

"I remember when people used to use it," my mother said,
"but it seems to've pretty much stopped now."

The twins shoved each other back and forth
in a dramatic interpretation of war
they'd first made popular at a third grade talent show.

In a quiet moment, I thought about my father as he'd looked
before he went off to fight
and the feeling I got when I'd found out he was dead.

Looking at pictures of him,
it was easy to see the logic of growth,
the developments in the face year to year,
all present in the earliest versions.
Yet, to predict what he'd have looked like now
was almost impossible,
except to say, "Just like this, only a little older,
a little wiser about the terrors of the world
and the relief at having woken up each morning
with only tennis elbow and moderate debt—
I mean, as opposed to the other thing.

The other thing is so much worse."

I REMEMBER WHEN THEY OPENED, ETC

I remember when they opened the Gaza Strip Club
amidst fanfare and protest in 1988—
or, Year of the Parent-Teacher Conference
according to this calendar for a religion
whose doctrine holds
that honesty is merely one of the policies
and the most important decisions are game-time decisions.

I was just eight, but already familiar with
the Let's Go Guide to American Castles

and a non-fiction epic called History of Sleep,
written by a man who described himself as an immigrant
despite having been born and raised
among the many articulate forests
of a Connecticut highway strip.

It was just about that time I had my first communion,
held at the Senior Citizen's Center
in a part of town known for its easy-to-read coinage
and a statue of the earliest known human
to have invested in term life insurance.

The priest called my name amidst the ambient noise
of Bingo and respirators,
mispronouncing it in a way that made it sound impossibly
    unfamiliar,
like the Welsh for anything
or the native word for a South American fish
that'd die instantly in our markedly colder waters.

It makes me think of how
there are places I'll never go—
be it oil rig or Namibia—
no matter how long I live.

And when I'm asked that question,
"Would you choose to live forever?"
I always answer yes, because there are
infinite stats to calculate each season,
like the Walk to Strikeout ratios of journeymen relievers
and the exact amount of depression I feel
whenever I'm asked to elaborate
on the strength and diversity of my investment portfolio.

It's always possible you could get your own sports radio show
and find out first hand
just how much players and coaches
want to put points up on the board.

"It's a struggle each time,
but we hope to play hard and get the W,"
they say at every turn
like the earliest models of robots
programmed for one task only.

But those are the robots I like.
And if there were a movie in which they took over the world,
I'd like that movie,
starring a little-known actor in his first leading role
who realizes that robots are just like us,
maybe not in how they look or talk,
but that they've got needs, too,
like processors that won't freeze up
and like dramatically wider sidewalks
along all these city streets
so there's room to walk two-by-two
with their larger robot bodies.

ALONE AFTER SCHOOL IN THOSE DAYS, ETC

Alone after school in those days,
in the era later known for its warmer, slimmer jacket designs,
I began to write the fake histories of non-extant cultures,
of a people in an Arctic village with nothing but middle names,
or another, off the coast of Arkansas,
whose voices so resembled thunderclaps
their dogs remained forever burrowed under the beds upstairs.

Amid my afternoon chores—
the walking of the dog,
the taking out of the trash,
full, as it was, with day-old racing programs—
I pieced together the rise-and-falls of tribe and state alike,
until the last discernible moments of their respective stories,
be it the sacking of a heretofore invincible city,
or an ancient language completely altered one night
when the chief of a South American people
purposely affected
what he thought to be a fashionable lisp.

In these histories, I refounded the inventions of the world:
the first team mascots in a place swarming with Trojans and Bruins,
the first literary critics in a dark land of ceaseless boredom,
and the original version of the Bible,
labeled Caution: Explicit Lyrics,
because it was all "knew" this and "knew" that.

I worked on them everyday until my mother got home from work
to share stories of the health insurance industry,
or of a new type of traffic accident
no one had thought of till this evening's commute.

"It began with a girl reading the funnies page
to everyone else in the car," she'd say,
"which doesn't even make sense,
because the funnies are anything but."

Meanwhile, I'd be conceiving of an early social document
called Diary of Certain Binge Drinkers

or of the first analgesics
available over-the-counter
but nevertheless claiming
to have a certain prescription strength.

INVECTIVE

Who let the hornet in
while I sat and wrote my poems?

Was it you,
Davey, Justin, and Michael?

So jealous,
you try to sabotage me
while I conceive of my charming scenarios.

Grass that knows two languages,
wind that memorizes poems:
that's what I was writing about!,
and all the other impossibilities.

Clearly, you're threatened by my talents.
But no matter:
I've killed the hornet
by reading your own poems outloud.

It struggled. It was brave.
But in the end
your verse was much too cruel.

You should feel good, actually:
your poems have a practical use—
as a strong insect repellant.

And maybe I'd wipe my ass with them, too,
if they weren't already so full of shit!

THREE UNIQUE CULTURAL ASPECTS

I
Nigerian trashtalk

II
Mayan handball court

III
Protestant barn

FOUR THEMES WITH ANDREW MISTER

The first attempt of the shuttle
to carve the apple in half
embarrassed everyone
like a girl with fog in her vagina
bringing up the topic of former girlfriends
while sitting with the damaged armor
of a man skinned alive
yelling for his father to see him this last once
without the suit of his flesh on
The second attempt reminded everyone
of their responsibility as humans
to protect each other from the elements
when a tornado rips a girl's mouth in half
or an earthquake shakes her breasts off
or a tidal wave knocks her pubic hair to the ground
or a hurricane shoves a painting in her face
of lovesick Tokyo
where buildings leave marks
on the sky
The third attempt was almost successful
like Wallace Stevens
with his mouth full of chestnuts
burning by the fire of his collected works
to bring heat to the starving minds
of the million pale-faced students
forced to write essays
about a strange flower
the sun
The fourth attempt is scheduled
for the same date as Horace's birthday
conveniently located near my own
on which I want nothing but my girlfriend back
not having kissed any Brazilians
I should know about
to love me and bring meaning to my life

like one who
quickly flipping the switch
gets under the covers
before the light has gone out
and the dream begins illuminated
by a fear I can't speak
but can only gesture at
alone as I've ever been
and needless to say

VISIONARY EXAMINATIONS

The particle of sunshine becomes a digit
on the calculator's face.
A black eye arrives at peak hours,
negating the proof of its invention.

                        *   *   *

Desert crept along the horizon
where the wall meets the floor of highway
and ceiling of stars.

                        *   *   *

Shower of dish cleaner,
the contagious morning light.
Various acts of the epode.

                        *   *   *

The goalie keeps time
by making tongue-clicks.
A monument is built
to imperfection.

                        *   *   *

She sang the anthem
of hands being washed.
A discography of
little-known events.

*   *   *

The mirror composes at will.
Halftime restores memory.
No one's as nervous
with their name on a list.

*   *   *

He had the dimples to store paper.
Tattered shreds of dinner.
The enemy hides his faults
in marginalia.

*   *   *

Troubleshooting for the new snow.
Symptoms become our only experience.

*   *   *

The mother's breast is made of aspartame.
The roots of the planted clock
send shivers up to
train tables.

*   *   *

Still Life with Account Info.
A policy suggests
future horror.

*   *   *

Pretty sight: dirt shoveled in the molasses.
A whistle goes to the border of its land.

*   *   *

Prelude to a Dream Vacation.
A shark's tooth makes deep logic.
Sand is the bullets' fist.

*   *   *

Don't attend
the statue's beard.

*   *   *

You'll go forever in one direction.

*   *   *

God as mighty as ibuprofen.

*   *   *

Nightmares make good epigraphs.

WE DROVE FOR HOURS, ETC

We drove for hours across dispassionate Kansas,
trading impersonations of the year's last snowfall
and thinking up jokes whose punchlines might include
the phrase "Pocket Awareness."

The land stretched out all around,
providing a host of metaphorical possibilities:

some about life, maybe,
"on account of the wide, bleak expanse"

and some about death, too,
"in terms of the wide, bleak expanse and whatnot."

Over the radio, between extreme rock hits of assorted decades,
we heard the breaking news of a shuttle tragedy
hundreds of miles away—
a distance which seemed much closer when we saw
this was only mere inches
on our road map of the United States.

We told each other the same story
of the same serial novelist
driving his truck into the same tornado,
only changing the intensity of the storm
and subsequent insurance claim
depending on our moods.

Later, at a roadside cafe,
we conceived of what would later become
our Duet on the Application of Neuroscience.
And though it was our only work,
we were forever championed by the critics
as pioneers of a Midwestern avant-garde.

Me, the one who could sketch
any five dictators in under a minute.
You, the one with a topspin backhand
and sapphires like two big eyes.

A CASSETTE TAPE OF HALLOWEEN SOUNDS, ETC

A cassette tape of Halloween sounds
is playing somewhere in my neighborhood
despite the fact it's a cold February day
and the children are all in snow pants
at the city's elementary schools
working out variations on the theme of kickball.

At home alone
I'm attempting to find a radio personality
to replace the real one I already have

but which has gotten me no further
than this small room of used or discount furniture
and a breakfast wholly indebted
to a food called "egg alternative."

This morning I had the joy of waking up
to a minor hangover,
which I call a joy
because it's just like being sick
except it goes away in a few hours
and the symptoms are all a direct result
of last night—

unlike a real illness
which, of course, is probably just a head cold
but could also be any number of horribly incurable maladies,
the nature of which stymies
even the most impressive physician.

In times like these
I play a game and guess where on the planet
dawn is happening
and what sort of adapter is required there
to use an electric razor.

I imagine myself
wandering the streets of this foreign destination,
mystified and slightly overwhelmed
by their exotic cultural practices,
like the main character of a film
whose preview I've seen again and again
but whose name I can't remember
and perhaps don't care to.

Better just to sit in one place, maybe,
and decode the almost infinite connotations
of a phrase like "This year's black"—

an idea which, at first glance,
reads like the earliest Roman calendars
which accounted for snowfall after snowfall
in the typically balmy month of September

but, after further investigation,
reveals the truth beyond a truth,
like a book of purportedly "Collected Letters,"
not only never collected,
but, in addition, never sent.

IT'S 1130A AND ONCE AGAIN, ETC

It's 1130a and once again I'm trying to remember
which sport is known as the "Sport of Kings"
and whether that's an actual phrase at all
or if I've just made it up once in a dream
and then brought it back with me to this side
like a sick friend smuggling
cheaper, potentially dirtier Mexican antibiotics
back to the US for another, comparatively sicker friend.

This won't be the day to do it,
but there's a day up there somewhere
which I might liken to an 800-number
with an excess of digits,
be it 1-800-TIRE-RAMA
or 1-800-COVERAGE

"For all your insurance needs."

I don't know what the day'll feel like
or even if it's sure to come,
but in terms of intellectual real estate
I feel I've cornered the market on this particular phenomenon
and I'm not afraid to use this minor victory as impetus
to while away the remainder of my afternoon
in search of talk radio which speaks directly to my personal crisis
or at least gets me through this next hour
of regularly scheduled programming.

And, this evening, when I've finally touched down
on my square of mattress,
I'll look back and title this all "A Minor Setback for Man,"
which could potentially be depressing
but because I'll have named it and given it a story

will be beautiful in the sad way
or sad in the beautiful way
but will, in either case, comfort me
like the passage from a French Cinema text book which reads:

"Because of the space between frames
and the closing of the projector's shutter,
almost fifty percent of any film experience
takes place completely in the dark."

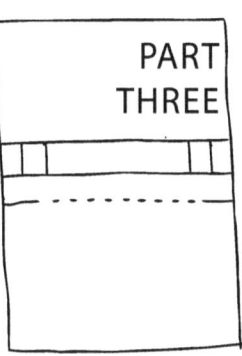

PART THREE

DIFFERENT POETS' AUDIENCES

The audience of Joe Hunt's poem
is people who need advice
on how to attain euphemism.

The audience of Bethany Bucholz's poem
is people who registered to vote
by knitting their eyebrows furiously.

For James Tate's poem,
it's people who carry shotguns
round their ankles.

For my flatmate Chris's poem,
it's people who call walking to the next room
real migratory behavior.

For Justin's,
it's people who talk even to kids
in academic German.

For the deceased Andre Breton's,
it's the orchestra that tells secrets
to a private alphabet.

And for that Joanna Klink's,
it can only be the corpses
we call women.

Meanwhile, the audience of my poem
is the people for whom a cherry bomb
goes straight to their thighs,
the people who leave very detailed instructions
on how they'll be remembered,
and those who sue their children
to recoup some of their losses.

If you want to know,
I dedicate it to anyone
whose name means yelping dog or US Postal Carrier,
or who has proof of when they'll die
besides just the normal ungainly fowl,
the darkling birds of home and office.

THE CHEERFUL LANDSLIDE

Evening rates are up this month
thanks to the Secretary of Bon Mots
who fondles his desk accessories
after the employees have gone home
by way of an escape-hatch-painted mural.
Belinda in Marketing wears a blouse
that exposes her umpire's whistle,
Courtney is a bitch for tearing out the notebook pages
on which I'd recorded a History of Tennis Elbow.
Terrible apparitions emerge:
a man calls "fore" at an approaching cold front,
a weatherman grows sleepy at the mention of apocalypse,
they've silent auctioned off my pen, my hand.
Last night I met the linguist Ilaria Frana
whose name in English is the title of this poem.
When James Tate reads it,
he'll know I've followed his sage-like offering:
"Carson, you're as tactful a person, as I am bad a poet."

BARELY FROM THE SLOVENIAN

Making your mouth into octagon
is well-known remedy for insatiable desire,
while into shape of pentagon
will benefit God and country.
Other shapes will have effects
like early human meeting future relative.
I regret to inform, there is no shape with only two sides.
"Why?" I asked my father, who for one year
was my age in "feet tall."
"Carson," he says, "eat your soup!"
For job in astronomy, economy, any-onomy,
make your mouth into shape
of concept "justice."
For metaphysics,
place mouth in shape of work-leisure dichotomy.
Do you know that bear lives in neighborhood?
I am telling you about it.
For Determinism,
put it so mouth resembles comeback win.
For a little amusement,
place mouth against "fuck" in dictionary.
For Ablative of Means,
do it this way, what is our word for "mouth-dance,"
but for Ablatives Agent and Otherwise,
do it this other one, more like "mouth-committed-suicide."
From now on, I think, it is not obligation
to direct film.
Place mouth in relief of anxiety!
You are a Connecticut Yankee?,
or a Connecticut Red Sox?, I can't tell.
Place mouth in regional controversy!
Even on street, or country road,
women undress in different languages,
it wouldn't be Feminism of me to "translate."

Desire cripples, a.k.a. Godard's film.
Which, this goes back to octagon:
eight sides for eight perfect batters.
Plus, Big Papi—as capital DH!

POSTGAME COMMENTS
BY CELTICS' CAPTAIN PAUL PIERCE
AS AN APPROACH TO THE CREATIVE PROCESS

People don't understand what
the game of poetry is all about
Pierce said it's
a physical war
but people don't understand
the psychology of the poetry
I was just trying to
get my poetry fired up
get my emotions into my
poetry and poetry
responded

MY FUTURE IN BUSINESS

So come on down to Cistulli's.

And let the folks at Cistulli's.

Find out why Cistulli's.

Cistulli's is waiting.

A LOREN GOODMAN POEM I WROTE TO AIMEE LEDUC FROM FOURTH GRADE YESTERDAY

Why didn't you say you were totally
crushing on me in November instead of
going out with Ryan Blazon in May?
He's nice, but I would've gone out with you,
I was crushing on you so hard and Kristy Hodgkins,
but Kristy's not in Spelling Book D, you are.
I mean, it's cool, I'm just bummed, Mrs Terry
said Rob's special, I'm not special, what a jerk.
Hey, what'd you write your story on. I wrote
on teen pregnancy. My dad says. My mom
says. Did you guys make out, really?

AMBASSADOR TO A LAVA LAMP, ETC

Ambassador to a Lava Lamp,
I have for X years admired your dress style
which is like a bear cub roaming the Tuleries.
I'm wondering, how long was the
astronaut in his mommy's tummy
before he could roast his own meat?
Hey, did you ever take science much?
I ask because we just dissected the dictator's hamstring:
I learned alot about society from it,
and maybe philosophy, I think.
At least it's better than the weeping of a microscope.
Anyway, take your wife from behind for me—
if she's still living, that is—
and gladly welcome summer,
that season best represented as
a corpse with lipstick.

TWO SONNETS

1
My hometown can beat up your hometown.
My god is crunker than your god.
I didn't necessarily embrace this poverty.
It was more like, I waved to it from across the street.

The directions say take a left here,
but to do so would necessitate death.
So either the directions are wrong
or they're just directing us to die.

The woman in the Expedition is a) laughing or b) crying.
She's a) topless or b) bottomless.
Which is it and why?

The woman in the Expedition is tantric and awesome.
She's got on base skills and slugging percentages.
On my gravestone, let it read: "If you lived here, you'd be home now."

2
On your mark, get set, go.
What's the prettiest word in the English language?
Don't know? Then what's the state with the most pride in it?
The answer's Connecticut. Next question.

At some point you'll die of a) cancer or b) heart disease.
For the former, turn to page 56.
For the latter, turn to your life partner.
Turn to her and go, "Holy crap."

A study suggests eat fruit, not breads, eat hearts, not livers.
My mom suggests don't wear that shirt with those pants.
Regardless, I have a weird, semi-permanent future.

Today, a grand jury found the defendant guilty on all counts.
Today, my sister found a toy in her cereal.
Hey, it's hilarious, guys: said "future," meant "fever."

from THE CONTEMPLATIVE'S JOKE BOOK

Q. What do you call a communion wafer that's Feminist?
A. Bread that breaks itself.

Q. What's a normal bedtime for the genius?
A. Refer yourself to the best formula.

Q. What's a normal bedtime for the genius?
A. Whenever the "greater than" decrees it.

Q. What do you get when you cross Justin with humility?
A. Hey, what'd you do with the real Justin? This isn't him. Is the real Justin okay? Did you take him?

Q. What do you get when you cross Josh Bolton with Talent?
A. The contingency is unlikely.

Q. What do you get when you cross Josh Bolton with Talent?
A. Let's cross that bridge when it's ever built.

Q. What's the description for Josh Bolton's aesthetic?
A. "Palimpsestic" would be a lesson in understatement.

Q. What's the description for Josh Bolton's aesthetic?
A. A date book full of non-starters.

Q. What's the description for Josh Bolton's aesthetic?
A. The Olympic event of Having It Up to Here.

Q. How does dandruff make its living?
A. Apparently my scalp is a good starting point.

Q. Where does a prostitute eat her meals?
A. In a William T. Vollman novel, is a good answer.

POPULAR SUPERSTITIONS

At the doctor's office:
touch your shin to all the paperwork.

Returning an overdue book:
offer your dry skin as payment instead.

When decorating the Christmas tree:
sing a hymn of the crap sandwich.

EXCUSE MY PURE PRAYER

A BB rises to the surface, like a splinter.
Don't ever let them call it a "minor"
heart attack: minor for whom?
Anytime you swim, someone drowns.
Last week, my dad went to get mail
and came back alive. He had a coupe once.
"A French car is one that's been cooked too long,"
is a German saying. 10,000 people
lose the same job. Thunder claps. Café au laits
are mores expensive here. Kali always
asks me to pay: "With what money?" I ask.
That's just one of our routines.
Is God a series of routines?
I sit here, waiting. At the Q & A
session, I gave the As before
Tomaz Salamun could. It was a thrill
meeting him in his official uniform.
Like horse bone, he holds no odor.
I'll work under the assumption
that I'm every character in my dreams:
minister of defense, learning to wag
his tail; Latin tutor, folding his
clothes into the shape of a question mark;
child learning the violin, whose youth
will be preserved by salt; financier,
positioned by the metaphysical cap gun;
architect, in special antidoping-cut jeans;
the clock itself, about to turn infinity o'clock;
the window, looking out onto the humanity
of paper clips; the eagle's talon, about to
seize the fish's Genius. I read a book
not to find its meaning, but to find my
happiness. I'm an ascetic now, tell mom.
I write a book On Mystery. In it, I finally learned:

it's okay to drink Italian sodas quickly.
There are more Italian sodas on the
horizon. What else is like that, I wonder?

A NOTE ON THE TYPE

The editors understand that, given the font's diminutive size, it may cause the eye some fatigue. This is no accident. Rather, it is a safety measure to prevent the reader from an excess of Cistulli's poems, which, in that case, would cause *fatigue of the heart*.

AUTHOR DATA

Name: Carson Cistulli
Born: December 23, 1979
Birthplace: Concord, NH
Education: B.A., Classical Civ—Univ of Montana

www.ingramcontent.com/pod-product-compliance
Lightning Source LLC
Chambersburg PA
CBHW032024040426
42448CB00006B/717